SCHOLASTIC

Grades 4–8

5-Minute MATH
Problem of the Day

Marcia Miller and Martin Lee

New York • Toronto • London • Auckland • Sydney
Mexico City • New Delhi • Hong Kong • Buenos Aires

For Jerry and Alan

Cover design by Niloufar Safavieh
Cover image: Syda Productions/Fotolia
Interior design by Solutions by Design, Inc.
Interior illustrations by Rick Brown

ISBN 978-0-439-17539-5

25 26 27 28 29   40   21 20 19 18 17

Contents

Introduction

D oesn't everyone love to find a solution to a problem? Kids certainly do. Most of them love challenges and will respond to them enthusiastically. Upon grasping a complex idea or successfully solving a thorny problem, they experience a special feeling of accomplishment.

Providing your students with motivating and challenging word problems, math puzzlers, and riddles will do more than give them the opportunity to feel good—it will help foster an active engagement in mathematics. The National Council of Teachers of Mathematics (NCTM) endorses this view in its *Principles and Standards for School Mathematics (Standards 2000)*. Active engagement in problem solving can fuel students' curiosity about mathematical ideas and encourage them to talk about those ideas.

According to the NCTM, the best kinds of problems are those that students can access on different levels and that challenge them in varied ways. Whether these problems are about things kids know from their own world, or are of a purely mathematical nature, what they have in common is that they get kids to think mathematically. They call upon students to apply their number sense and intuitive thinking skills, make and test reasonable estimates, adjust assumptions, explore patterns, use proportional reasoning and algebraic ideas, work backwards, draw sketches or diagrams, use manipulatives, or even act out situations. Optimal problems require kids to combine conceptual understanding with procedural proficiency. They provide kids with the opportunity to prepare for what they will need to do as adults—use math reasoning and quantitative skills to solve the everyday problems, mental calculations, and estimations they will face as citizens and in the workplace.

The math curriculum for grades 4–8 contains interconnected and overlapping ideas. Therefore, it is difficult to neatly divide these concepts into separate content units. In this book, for ease of use, we have arranged the problems into seven broad groupings. Within each grouping, and on each page, the problems, many of which integrate multiple concepts, are generally ordered from easiest to most difficult.

We hope you'll find that the word problems, puzzlers, and riddles in *5-Minute Math Problem of the Day* engage your students, enrich your math curriculum, and contribute to your goal of creating a classroom in which mathematical thinking is central.

Connection With the NCTM Standards 2000

	Number and Operations	Algebra	Geometry	Measurement	Data Analysis and Probability	Problem Solving	Reasoning and Proof*	Communication*	Connections*	Representation*
Whole Numbers										
Place Value	X					X	X	X	X	X
Comparing & Ordering Numbers	X					X	X	X	X	X
Rounding	X					X	X	X	X	X
Sums & Differences	X					X	X	X	X	X
Adding & Multiplying	X	X				X	X	X	X	X
Number Patterns	X	X				X	X	X	X	X
Multiplying & Dividing	X	X				X	X	X	X	X
Estimating Sums & Differences	X					X	X	X	X	X
Divisibility	X					X	X	X	X	X
Factors & Multiples	X	X			X	X	X	X	X	X
Decimals										
Place Value	X					X	X	X	X	X
Rounding	X					X	X	X	X	X
Sums & Differences	X	X			X	X	X	X	X	X
Operations With Money	X	X				X	X	X	X	X
Multiplying & Dividing	X	X				X	X	X	X	X
Fractions										
Fraction Concepts	X					X	X	X	X	X
Equivalent Fractions	X	X				X	X	X	X	X
Density Property	X					X	X	X	X	X
Sums & Differences	X	X				X	X	X	X	X
Mixed Operations	X	X			X	X	X	X	X	X

* Standard can be met by using many of the Teacher Tips found on page 8.

Connection With the NCTM Standards 2000

	Number and Operations	Algebra	Geometry	Measurement	Data Analysis and Probability	Problem Solving	Reasoning and Proof*	Communication*	Connections*	Representation*
Measurement										
Coin Problems	X	X		X			X	X	X	X
Customary Units	X	X		X			X	X	X	X
Perimeter & Area	X	X		X			X	X	X	X
Measurement With Fun Facts	X	X		X			X	X	X	X
Time Zones	X	X		X			X	X	X	X
Multi-Step Problems	X	X		X	X		X	X	X	X
Geometry										
Angles & Clocks			X	X			X	X	X	X
Angles & Polygons		X	X	X			X	X	X	X
Angles & Figures			X	X			X	X	X	X
Surface Area		X	X	X			X	X	X	X
Pythagorean Theorem	X	X	X	X			X	X	X	X
Percents, Ratio, & Probabillity										
Percents, Fractions, & Decimals	X						X	X	X	X
Percents & Measurement	X	X		X			X	X	X	X
Percents & Discounts	X	X		X	X		X	X	X	X
Ratio & Proportion	X	X		X	X		X	X	X	X
Counting Principle	X						X	X	X	X
Probability	X						X	X	X	X
Algebra & Statistics										
Patterns	X	X					X	X	X	X
Equations	X	X		X			X	X	X	X
Averages	X	X			X		X	X	X	X
Integers	X	X		X			X	X	X	X
Squares & Square Roots	X	X					X	X	X	X

* Standard can be met by using many of the Teacher Tips found on page 8.

Teacher Tips

◎ Not every word problem, puzzler, or riddle is appropriate for every class. Pick and choose as you see fit. Feel free to adapt or adjust problems to suit the interests and ability levels of your students.

◎ Use the problems as warm-ups to open your math class, as problems of the day, or as part of homework assignments. If you assign them as homework, encourage parents to pitch in.

◎ Assign one or two problems at a time. You may wish to copy individual problems onto the board or overhead projector, post them on a bulletin board, present them orally, or set up a grab-bag system where your students take turns picking the "surprise" problem each day.

◎ Each page of problems is fully reproducible. To reinforce specific math concepts, you can copy and distribute the whole page to use as classroom practice, homework, or even a quiz.

◎ Set up a number-detective *beat* that your *sleuths* can check each day. Provide different math resource materials such as reference books, tables, graph paper, and rulers, as well as clues—written suggestions left behind by fellow students indicating different ways to approach a particular problem. You can fill out a "Certificate of Recognition" (reproducible provided on page 64) to recognize the efforts of each sleuth.

◎ As needed, ask guiding questions, give hints, and aim students in the right direction if they have trouble getting a handle on a problem.

◎ Many problems lend themselves to collaboration. Invite students to pair up or work in small groups. Have students share their solution methods and mathematical thinking. Encourage discussion, acknowledgement, and respect for diverse strategies and approaches. Feel free to determine the best grouping to suit your own teaching style and the learning styles of your students.

◎ Encourage students to record their calculations, solution plans, and sketches in their math logs. Some problems and their solutions may be appropriate for inclusion in students' portfolios.

◎ Have students make up their own word problems, puzzlers, and riddles for classmates to solve. Students can post these in the classroom math center, resource area, or on an online problem-solvers' bulletin board.

◎ Take the time to tackle the problems yourself. Students will benefit from seeing you in the role of a problem-solver.

Place Value

Use the digits in the box to answer each number riddle.
You cannot repeat digits within a number.

1 2 3 4 5 6 7 8 9

  I am the largest 4-digit odd number you can make.

What number am I? _____

  I am the smallest 5-digit even number you can make.

What number am I? _____

  I am the largest 5-digit even number you can make that has a 3 in the thousands place.

What number am I? _____

  I am the smallest 5-digit number you can make that has all odd digits.

What number am I? _____

  I am the largest 6-digit number you can make that has a 1 in the thousands place and a 5 in the ten-thousands place.

What number am I? _____

  I am the smallest 6-digit even number you can make that has a 6 in the hundreds place.

What number am I? _____

Place Value

7

I am a 4-digit number. My ones digit is 2. My tens digit is 4 greater than my ones digit. My hundreds and thousands digits are both 3 greater than my ones digit.

What number am I? _____

8

I am a 4-digit number greater than 9,000. My ones digit is 3 and my hundreds digit is the smallest prime number greater than 5. The sum of my digits is 20.

What number am I? _____

9

I am a 5-digit number greater than 30,000 and less than 40,000. My first and last digits are the same. The sum of my thousands, hundreds, and tens digits is 15. My tens digit is 4 times as great as my hundreds digit.

What number am I? _____

10

I am a number greater than 40,000 and less than 60,000. My ones digit and tens digit are the same. My ten-thousands digit is 1 less than 3 times the sum of my ones digit and tens digit. My thousands digit is half my hundreds digit, and the sum of those two digits is 9.

What number am I? _____

Comparing & Ordering Numbers

Use the digits in the box to answer each number riddle.
You cannot repeat digits within a number.

1 8 3 4 9 6 2 7

I am the number that is 100 greater than 3,362.

What number am I? _____

I am the number that is 40 less than the largest number you can make using five of the digits.

What number am I? _____

I am the largest number you can make that is greater than 8,745 but less than 8,750.

What number am I? _____

I am the number that is 5,000 greater than the smallest number you can make using six of the digits.

What number am I? _____

I am the smallest number you can make that is greater than 617,500.

What number am I? _____

I am the largest number you can make that is less than 618,400 but greater than 618,300.

What number am I? _____

Rounding

 We are the smallest and largest whole numbers that round to 70 when rounded to the nearest ten.

What numbers are we?_____

 We are the smallest and largest whole numbers that round to 600 when rounded to the nearest hundred.

What numbers are we?_____

 We are the smallest and largest whole numbers that round to 8,000 when rounded to the nearest thousand.

What numbers are we?_____

 We are the smallest and largest whole numbers that round to 90,000 when rounded to the nearest ten-thousand.

What numbers are we?_____

 We are the smallest and largest whole numbers that round to 70,000 when rounded to the nearest thousand.

What numbers are we?_____

 We are the smallest and largest whole numbers that round to 170,000 when rounded to the nearest ten-thousand.

What numbers are we?_____

5-Minute Math Problem of the Day Scholastic Professional Books

Rounding

23 The sum of my digits is 11. When rounded to the nearest hundred, I am 500. Rounding to the nearest ten makes me 530.

What number am I? _____

24 When rounded to the nearest thousand, I round to 3,000. Rounding to the nearest hundred makes me 2,700. Three of my digits are the same.

What number am I? _____

25 To the nearest ten-thousand, I round to 80,000. I round to 81,000 when rounded to the nearest thousand, and to 81,200 when rounded to the nearest hundred. To the nearest ten, I round to 81,220. I am a palindrome, too.

What number am I? _____

26 Rounding me to the nearest ten, hundred, thousand, or ten-thousand will give you the same number. Four of my digits are the same. The sum of all five of my digits is 39.

What number am I? _____

Sums & Differences

Use the digits in the box to answer each number riddle. Digits appear only once in an answer. Each answer may not use all digits.

2 4 9 6 7 3

 When you subtract a 2-digit number from a 3-digit number, the difference is 473.

What are the numbers? _____

 The sum of these two numbers is 112.

What are the numbers? _____

 The sum of these two numbers is 519.

What are the numbers? _____

 The difference between these two 3-digit numbers is 263.

What are the numbers? _____

 The sum of these three 2-digit numbers is 184.

What are the numbers? _____

 The difference between two 3-digit numbers is a palindrome between 200 and 300.

What are the numbers? _____

5-Minute Math Problem of the Day Scholastic Professional Books

Sums & Differences

33

Point-scoring in the Inter-Galaxy Football League

Touchdown . . . . 6 points
Touchdown with an extra point . . . . 7 points
Touchdown with a 2-point conversion . . . . 8 points
Field Goal . . . . 3 points

The Asteroids played the Constellations. Each team scored a field goal in the first quarter. In the second quarter, the Asteroids scored a touchdown, but missed the extra point. At the half, the Constellations led by 1 point. In the third quarter, the Asteroids made a touchdown with the extra point. The Constellations matched them, and made a field goal, as well. In the fourth quarter, following a Constellation field goal, the Asteroids scored a touchdown with a 2-point conversion.

Who won? _____

By what score? _____

34

Point-scoring in the Inter-Galaxy Basketball League consists of 1-point free throws, 2-point goals, 3-point goals, and 4-point goals (those made without looking at the basket!).

The Comets, playing the Meteors, led 22–9 at the end of the first quarter. They led by 7 at the half after scoring two 4-point goals, two 3-point goals, four 2-point goals, and three free throws. In the third quarter, the Meteors had six 2-point goals and four free throws. They also had one more 4-point goal, but one less 3-point goal than the Comets. The Comets had five 2-point goals and no free-throws. They scored 20 points in the quarter. In the last quarter, each team scored the same number of 4-point, 3-point, and 2-point goals. The Comets scored 31 points in that quarter, including four free throws. The Meteors made two fewer free throws than the Comets.

Who won? _____

By what score? _____

Adding & Multiplying

35 Two counting numbers are three apart. Their sum is 47.

What are the numbers? _____

36 The product of two consecutive numbers is 210.

What are the numbers? _____

37 The sum of two twin primes is 60.

What are the numbers? _____

38 Three consecutive numbers have a sum of 135.

What are the numbers? _____

39 The product of three consecutive odd numbers is 6,783.

What are the numbers? _____

40 Two numbers have a product of 676 and a quotient of 4.

What are the numbers? _____

5-Minute Math Problem of the Day Scholastic Professional Books

Number Patterns

 41 I am the seventh number in the following sequence of numbers: 1, 4, 9, 16, …

What number am I? _____

 42 I am the sixth number in the following sequence of numbers: 1, 3, 7, 15, …

What number am I? _____

 43 Edgar does sit-ups daily. On Monday, he did 20 sit-ups. On Tuesday, he did 30. He did 50 sit-ups on Wednesday, and 90 on Thursday. If he continues this pattern, Edgar will do an impressive number of sit-ups on Saturday.

What number of sit-ups will he do? _____

44 Attendance at the National Typewriter Show has been decreasing each year. It was 2,000 in 1998; 1,985 in 1999; 1,940 in 2000; and 1,805 in 2001. If the drop-off continues at the same rate, one year soon, no one will attend.

What year will that be? _____

Number Patterns

· · · · · · · · · · · · · · ·

Follow the steps to find the mystery quotient.

45 Choose three different 1-digit numbers. Write all the 2-digit numbers you can using the three numbers. Then add these six 2-digit numbers. Next, find the sum of your original three numbers. Then divide the sum of the six numbers by the sum of the three numbers. Finally, repeat all these steps for another set of three 1-digit numbers, then again for a third set.

What is the quotient each time? _____

46 Repeat all the steps to find the mystery quotient above, but this time start with *four* different 1-digit numbers. (Note that now you will be able to make twelve 2-digit numbers.) Again, check your quotient by starting with two other sets of numbers.

What is this quotient each time? _____

47 Suppose that you followed all the steps above for *five* different 1-digit numbers. Make a prediction.

What will the quotient be? _____

48 Suppose you were to follow all the steps above for *six* different 1-digit numbers. Make a prediction.

What will the quotient be? _____

5-Minute Math Problem of the Day Scholastic Professional Books

Multiplying & Dividing

Using the digits in the box, write the answer to each number riddle in the form of an equation. Digits appear only once in an answer.

8 1 4 7 3

The product of a 1-digit number and a 2-digit number is 284.

What are the numbers? _____

The product of two 2-digit numbers, plus a number, is 3,355.

What are the numbers? _____

The product of a 3-digit number and a 1-digit number, minus another 1-digit number, is 1,137.

What are the numbers? _____

The product of a 2-digit number and a 3-digit number is between 13,000 and 14,000.

What are the numbers? _____

When a 3-digit number is divided by a 2-digit number, the quotient is between 5 and 6.

What are the numbers? _____

When a 2-digit prime number is divided by another 2-digit prime number, the quotient is nearly 5.

What are the numbers? _____

Estimating Sums & Differences

55 When two whole numbers are each rounded to the nearest ten, the sum is 80. One of the addends is the greatest number that rounds to 30. The second addend is the least number it can be.

What is the sum of the two numbers? _____

56 The sum of two whole numbers, each rounded to the nearest hundred, is 7,000. One addend rounds to 3,400. The other addend is the largest whole number it can be.

What number is it? _____

57 Rounded to the nearest hundred, the sum of two numbers is 11,000. Each addend is the greatest number it can be. One addend has 4 digits and the other has 3 digits.

What are the numbers? _____

58 If two numbers are each rounded to the nearest thousand, their sum is 50,000 and their difference is 10,000. Each is the greatest number it can be, given those conditions.

What are the numbers? _____

20

Divisibility

 59 I am a 2-digit number. The sum of my digits is 11. I am divisible by both 4 and 7.

What number am I? _____

 60 I am a 2-digit number divisible by 4, 6, and 7.

What number am I? _____

 61 I am a 2-digit number divisible by 19. The sum of my digits is 14.

What number am I? _____

 62 I am a 3-digit number divisible by 7, but not 2. The sum of my digits is 4.

What number am I? _____

 63 I am a 3-digit number less than 300. I am divisible by 2 and 5, but not 3. The sum of my digits is 7.

What number am I? _____

 64 I am a 3-digit number divisible by 3. My tens digit is 3 times as great as my hundreds digit, and the sum of my digits is 15. If you reverse my digits, I am divisible by 6, as well as by 3.

What number am I? _____

Factors & Multiples

65

I am a number less than 40. One of my factors is 7. The sum of my digits is 8.

What number am I? _____

66

I am a number less than 100. Two of my factors are 3 and 5. My digits are 1 apart.

What number am I? _____

67

I am a number less than 60. Two of my factors are 2 and 7. I am a common multiple of 8 and 14.

What number am I? _____

68

I am a common multiple of 2 and 5. I am also a factor of 100. The sum of my digits is 5.

What number am I? _____

69

I am a factor of 120, and a common multiple of 3, 4, and 10. The sum of my digits is 6.

What number am I? _____

70

I am a 2-digit number greater than 50. One of my factors is 8 and I, myself, am a factor of 360. The difference between my digits is 5.

What number am I? _____

5-Minute Math Problem of the Day Scholastic Professional Books

Factors & Multiples

71 I am the least common multiple of two numbers whose sum is 27 and whose difference is 3.

What are the two numbers?_____

What number am I? _____

72 I am the least common multiple of two numbers whose sum is 20. One number is 4 greater than the other.

What are the two numbers?_____

What number am I? _____

73 I am the greatest common factor of two numbers whose sum is 24 and whose difference is 6.

What are the two numbers?_____

What number am I? _____

74 I am the greatest common factor of three numbers. Their sum is 36. The largest number is twice the smallest and the middle number is the mean of the other two.

What are the three numbers? _____

What number am I? _____

Factors & Multiples

75

The Eggplant Avenue bus passes Max's house every 8 minutes. The Cabbage Creek bus passes it every 12 minutes. The two buses last passed by together at 9:00 AM.

When is the next time that will happen? _____

76

The Allentown train passes every 20 minutes. The Bard train passes every 15 minutes. The Carlton train passes every 18 minutes. It is 6:00 PM and all three just passed by.

When is the next time that will happen? _____

77

I am the fewest number of armadillos that meets the following conditions: When grouped by twos, by threes, or by fours, there is one left over. When grouped by fives, there are none left over.

What number am I? _____

78

I am the fewest number of fish that meets the following conditions: When netted by threes, by fours, or by fives, there is one left over.

What number am I? _____

Place Value

Rearrange the digits and the decimal point in the box to find your answer. Use each digit in every answer. If your answer is less than 1, be sure to place a zero in the ones place.

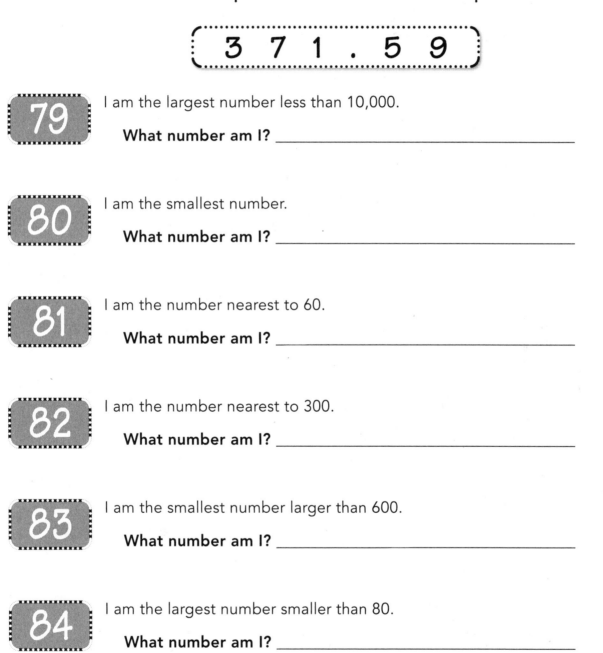

```
3  7  1  .  5  9
```

79 I am the largest number less than 10,000.

What number am I? _____

80 I am the smallest number.

What number am I? _____

81 I am the number nearest to 60.

What number am I? _____

82 I am the number nearest to 300.

What number am I? _____

83 I am the smallest number larger than 600.

What number am I? _____

84 I am the largest number smaller than 80.

What number am I? _____

Rounding

I am the largest number that rounds to 5.61 to the nearest hundredth.

What number am I? _____

I am the largest number that rounds to 4.717 to the nearest thousandth.

What number am I? _____

I am the smallest number that rounds to 0.62 to the nearest hundredth.

What number am I? _____

I am the smallest number that rounds to 50.306 to the nearest thousandth.

What number am I? _____

I am the largest number that rounds to 241.699 to the nearest thousandth.

What number am I? _____

I am the smallest number that rounds to 0.6444 to the nearest ten-thousandth.

What number am I? _____

5-Minute Math Problem of the Day Scholastic Professional Books

Rounding

 Rounding to the nearest whole number makes me 4. Rounding to the nearest tenth makes me 4.2. When I am rounded to the nearest hundredth, I am 4.23. I am the greatest number carried out to the thousandths place that meets all these conditions.

What number am I? _____

 Rounding to the nearest whole number makes me 13. Rounding to the nearest tenth makes me 12.6. Rounding to the nearest hundredth makes me 12.58. I am the greatest number carried out to the thousandths place that meets all these conditions.

What number am I? _____

 Rounding to the nearest whole number makes me 115. Rounding to the nearest tenth makes me 114.9. When I am rounded to the nearest hundredth, I am 114.93. I am the least number carried out to the thousandths place that meets all these conditions.

What number am I? _____

 Rounding to the nearest tenth makes me 203.5. Rounding to the nearest hundredth makes me 203.46. The sum of my digits is 15. Carry me out to the thousandths place.

What number am I? _____

Sums & Differences

 A train goes from Inchworm to Firefly, making stops along the way at Bumble Bee and at Humbug. The journey is 24 miles long. It is 4.8 miles from Bumble Bee to Humbug, and 7.6 miles from Humbug to Firefly.

How far from Inchworm to Humbug? _____

 The Sea Breeze Special starts at Tuna and stops at Salmon and Carp on its way to Trout. It is 18.4 km from Tuna to Salmon. The distance between Salmon and Trout is 26.5 km. The train makes the round trip in 44 minutes.

How far is the round trip?_____

 A train stops at the towns of Ouch, Hey, and No Way on its way to Whoa. Ouch is 22.2 miles west of No Way. No Way is 9.9 miles east of Hey. Hey is 13.7 miles west of Whoa.

How far is Whoa from Ouch?_____

Choose one number from each box to find your answer.

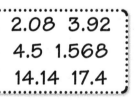
2.08 3.92
4.5 1.568
14.14 17.4

6.86 0.75 12.6 21.2 38.07 13.5

 Two numbers have a sum of 25.12.

What are the numbers? _____

 Two numbers have a difference of 7.28.

What are the numbers? _____

 Two numbers have a sum of 18 and a difference that is half of that.

What are the numbers? _____

Operations With Money

101 A jacket costs $100.00 more than a sweater. Together, they sell for $211.00.

What is the price of the jacket? _____

What is the price of the sweater? _____

102 At Nose for Clothes, Inez bought a T-shirt for $12.50 and a pair of jeans for $5.00 more than twice that price. She paid with a $50.00 bill.

What change should she get? _____

103 Ted and Charlene sold homemade chocolate chip cookies. After 5 days, they had sales totaling $40.00. Each day their sales were $0.25 higher than on the previous day.

What were sales on the first day? _____

104 Tanya brought $9.05 to the mall. She returned home with less than $1.00 in her purse.

What is the least she could have spent? _____

Multiplying & Dividing

Choose one number from the triangle and one from the circle to answer each question.

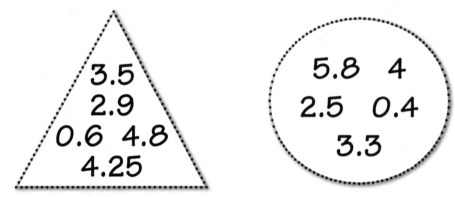

105 Two numbers have a product of 8.75.

What are the numbers? _____

106 Two numbers have a product of 17.

What are the numbers? _____

107 Two numbers have a product that is less than 1.

What are the numbers? _____

108 Two numbers have a product that is greater than 25.

What are the numbers? _____

5-Minute Math Problem of the Day Scholastic Professional Books

Fraction Concepts

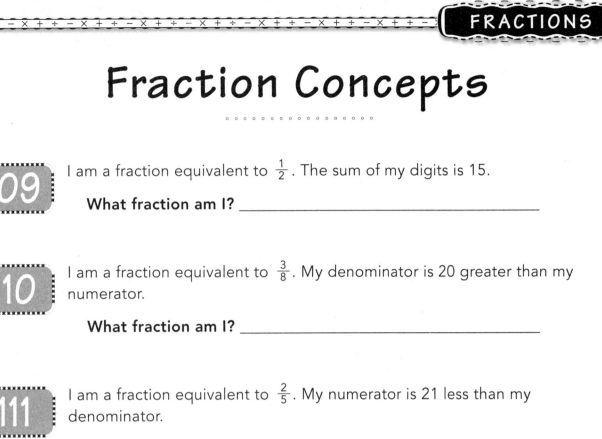

109 I am a fraction equivalent to $\frac{1}{2}$. The sum of my digits is 15.

What fraction am I? _____

110 I am a fraction equivalent to $\frac{3}{8}$. My denominator is 20 greater than my numerator.

What fraction am I? _____

111 I am a fraction equivalent to $\frac{2}{5}$. My numerator is 21 less than my denominator.

What fraction am I? _____

112 I am a fraction equivalent to $\frac{45}{60}$. If you were to multiply my denominator by my numerator, the product would be 192.

What fraction am I? _____

113 I am a fraction whose numerator and denominator are both prime numbers less than 20. If you were to increase each term by 1, I would be equivalent to $\frac{1}{2}$.

What fraction am I? _____

114 I am a fraction in simplest form. I am greater than $\frac{4}{5}$. The sum of my terms is 25.

What fraction am I? _____

Equivalent Fractions

To solve these puzzlers, you may use numbers more than once.

 Use the numbers 3, 12, and 6 to create two fractions that are equivalent to $\frac{1}{2}$.

What are the fractions? _____

 Use two prime numbers to create a fraction that is equivalent to $\frac{21}{49}$.

What is the fraction? _____

 Use the numbers 3 and 12 and one other whole number to create two fractions that are equivalent to $\frac{1}{4}$.

What are the fractions? _____

 Use the numbers 9 and 15 and one other whole number to create two fractions that are equivalent to $\frac{3}{5}$.

What are the fractions? _____

 Use the number 8 and two other whole numbers to create two fractions that are equivalent to $\frac{2}{3}$.

What are the fractions? _____

 Use the number 4 and two other whole numbers to create two fractions that are equivalent to $\frac{1}{2}$. Then do it another way.

What are the fractions? _____

5-Minute Math Problem of the Day Scholastic Professional Books

Density Property

 I am a fraction between $\frac{1}{8}$ and $\frac{1}{4}$. The sum of my digits is 10.

What fraction am I? _____

 I am a fraction between $\frac{1}{3}$ and $\frac{1}{5}$. My denominator is 1 less than 4 times my numerator.

What fraction am I? _____

 I am the smallest fraction between $\frac{2}{3}$ and $\frac{3}{4}$ with a numerator that is 7 less than my denominator.

What fraction am I? _____

 I am a fraction between $\frac{7}{8}$ and $\frac{11}{12}$. My denominator is $\frac{1}{2}$ the product of the denominators of the other two fractions.

What fraction am I? _____

 I am a mixed number between $1\frac{3}{4}$ and $1\frac{5}{6}$. The denominator of my fraction part is equal to the product of the denominators of the fraction parts of the other two mixed numbers.

What mixed number am I? _____

 I am a mixed number between $4\frac{5}{6}$ and $4\frac{2}{3}$. The numerator of my fraction part is equal to the sum of the digits of the lesser of the other two mixed numbers. The denominator of my fraction part is the least common multiple of 4 and 6.

What mixed number am I? _____

Sums & Differences

In each answer below, use the digits given, fraction bars, and either a plus sign or a minus sign.

 The solution is $\frac{5}{8}$. The digits are 1, 1, 2, and 8.

What is the problem? _____

 The solution is $\frac{1}{8}$. The digits are 5, 4, 3, and 8.

What is the problem? _____

 The solution is $\frac{1}{3}$. The digits are 1, 3, 4, and 6.

What is the problem? _____

 The solution is 1. The digits are 3, 10, 4, and 5.

What is the problem? _____

 The solution is $\frac{1}{4}$. The digits are 8, 3, 8, and 4.

What is the problem? _____

 The solution is $\frac{1}{4}$. The digits are 1, 6, 9, 5, and 2.

What is the problem? _____

5-Minute Math Problem of the Day Scholastic Professional Books

Mixed Operations

 133 One-half of a number added to one-fourth of 96 is 30.

What is the number? _____

 134 If you triple a number you will have one-half the number of hours in two days.

What is the number? _____

 135 If you double a number, you will get the same as the triple of one-fourth of 24.

What is the number? _____

 136 If you subtract a number from the square of 7 you will get one-fourth the product of 9 and 8.

What is the number? _____

 137 One-fifth of a number, subtracted from 20, is the same as one-fourth of 32.

What is the number? _____

 138 Think of two numbers whose greatest common factor is 12. If you divide the lesser of the two numbers by that greatest common factor, you get one-sixteenth of the other number.

What are the numbers? _____

Mixed Operations

Choose fractions or mixed numbers from the box to answer the questions that follow. Use numbers as often as needed.

$$\frac{3}{4} \qquad \frac{9}{10} \qquad \frac{2}{3} \qquad 2\frac{1}{2} \qquad \frac{4}{5} \qquad \frac{1}{6} \qquad \frac{1}{4}$$

139 Two numbers have a sum of $2\frac{1}{4}$.

What are the numbers? _____

140 Two numbers have a difference of $\frac{5}{12}$.

What are the numbers? _____

141 Two numbers have a sum of $\frac{11}{12}$.

What are the numbers? _____

142 Two numbers have a product of $\frac{3}{5}$.

What are the numbers? _____

143 Two numbers have a difference of $1\frac{1}{3}$.

What are the numbers? _____

144 Two numbers have a quotient of $\frac{8}{9}$.

What are the numbers? _____

5-Minute Math Problem of the Day Scholastic Professional Books

Mixed Operations

 145 Juan is less than 10 years old. He is one-half as old as Suki. In 8 years, Juan will be three-fourths as old as Suki.

How old is Juan? _____

 146 On a balance scale, a whole block balances a $\frac{3}{4}$-pound weight and three-fourths of a block.

What does a whole block weigh? _____

 147 Teresa gave two-thirds of her peanuts to Gabe. Then she gave one-half of the remaining peanuts to Carlos. She had 10 peanuts left.

How many did she begin with? _____

 148 A turkey weighs 10 pounds plus half of its weight.

What does it weigh? _____

Coin Problems

149 Anna has 15 coins in her purse. All are nickels and dimes. They total $1.35.

How many of each does she have?_____

150 Royce has $1.30 in dimes and quarters. He has one-fourth as many quarters as dimes.

How many of each does he have?_____

151 Letty has $5 in nickels, dimes, and quarters. She has 3 times as many nickels as dimes. She has 5 times as much money in quarters as she does in nickels.

How many of each does she have?_____

152 Five dollars is divided continuously among three boys. The first boy always gets $.02, the second boy always gets $.03, and the third always gets $.05, until all the money is gone.

How much money does each boy get?_____ _____

Customary Units

I am the number of inches
in the difference between
2 feet and 2 yards.

What number am I? _____

I am the number of tons in 5,000 pounds.

What number am I? _____

I am the number of ounces in a quarter-ton.

What number am I? _____

I am the difference between the number of minutes in an hour and a half,
and the number of seconds in a minute and a half.

What number am I? _____

I am the number of cups in a half-gallon plus the number of gallons equal to
24 pints.

What number am I? _____

I am the difference between the number of inches in a quarter-mile and the
number of inches in 880 yards.

What number am I? _____

Perimeter & Area

159

A rectangle has a perimeter of 150 inches. Its length is 4 times its width.

What are its dimensions? _____

160

The length of the longest side of a triangle is double that of the next longest side and 19 cm greater than the shortest side. The perimeter of the triangle is 41 cm.

How long is the shortest side? _____

161

A square has the same number of feet in its perimeter as there are square feet in its area.

How long is a side? _____

162

Granny Brown had a square piece of land measuring 100 yards on a side. She gave her son a square with an area of 3,600 square yards. She kept a square piece measuring 40 yards on a side for herself. She gave the remaining land to her two grandchildren, dividing it equally between them. She then told the grandchildren the area of the piece of land each would receive.

How big was each piece? _____

Measurement With Fun Facts

 In 1983, the world's lowest temperature was recorded in Antarctica. In degrees Fahrenheit, the thermometer dropped to 160 degrees below freezing.

What was the temperature? _____

 The world's longest foot race took place in1929. It took the winner 11 weeks, 48 hours to complete the 3,665-mile New York-to-Los Angeles event.

How many days did it take him? _____

 In California, the difference between one roller coaster's base and its highest peak is 1 foot higher than 138 yards.

How many feet is the drop? _____

 The world's heaviest hailstone fell in Bangladesh in 1986. It weighed $716\frac{1}{2}$ ounces less than the world's heaviest domestic cat: an Australian tabby that tipped the scales at 46 pounds, $15\frac{1}{2}$ ounces.

What did the hailstone weigh? _____

Time Zones

167 From his living room in Hoboken, New Jersey, Benny watched a ballgame played in Denver, Colorado. When the 3-hour game, which began there at 7:40 PM, ended, Benny turned off his TV set. He looked at his watch.

What time was it in New Jersey? _____

168 The Rosen family, from Chicago, Illinois, flew to visit cousins in Chico, California. The 3-hour, 45-minute flight left O'Hare Airport at 9:15 AM. It landed on schedule in Chico. Mr. Rosen looked at a clock in the terminal.

What time was it in California?_____

169 Including stops for food and gas, Eva averaged 58 miles per hour in her drive from New Orleans, Louisiana, to her grandmother's house near Miami, Florida, a distance of 870 miles. She left at noon and stopped one other time along the way—for a 4-hour nap at a rest stop. When she pulled into her grandmother's driveway, she read the clock on her dashboard.

What time was it in Florida? _____

170 An airplane heading for New York left Seattle, Washington, 1 hour, 30 minutes later than the scheduled departure time of 6:30 AM. Melvin was a passenger on the plane. Fortunately, the pilot was able to shave half an hour off the usual flight time of 6 hours, 20 minutes. From the time the plane landed, it took Melvin 40 minutes to get his luggage and get into a cab. The taxi driver looked at Melvin, then at her watch, and jotted down the time on her log.

What time was it in New York?_____

Multi-Step Problems

Use the information in the box to solve the problems.

Daily Rates $32.95 per day, 500 free miles (may be used any day of the week)
Weekend Rates $40.00 per day, 1,000 free miles (must include at least one weekend day)
Extra Charges Road Love Rentals charges each customer $0.15 a mile for every mile driven over the number of free miles. It puts 10 gallons of gas in the tank. If the car is returned with less than 10 gallons, the customer pays $1.50 per gallon. If the car is returned with more than 10 gallons, Road Love refunds the customer at the same rate.

 Simon rented at daily rates for 2 days. He drove 455 miles. He returned the car with 8 gallons of gas in the tank.

What was the rental cost?_____

 Sandra rented at weekend rates. She drove 1,250 miles over a 3-day weekend. She returned the car with 11 gallons of gas.

What was the rental cost?_____

 The Cho family wants to rent a car for 5 days. They plan to drive 1,500 miles.

Which plan is best for them?_____

 The Lopez family rented a car for 3 days. They drove it 1,100 miles and returned the vehicle with 8.5 gallons of gas. The bill came to $191.10.

Which plan did they use? _____

Angles & Clocks

The minute hand of a clock passes the hour hand several times between 3:00 PM and 3:00 AM.

How many times? _____

The hands of a clock form a straight angle at 6:00 PM.

At what time will that happen next? _____

The hands of a clock form a right angle at 3:00 AM.

At what time will that happen next? _____

From noon to midnight, the hands of a clock form straight angles several times.

How many times? _____

5-Minute Math Problem of the Day Scholastic Professional Books

Angles & Polygons

179 In triangle *ABC*, the degree measure of angle *A* is 20° greater than the degree measure of angle *B*. Angle *C* is a right angle.

What is the measure of ∠ B? _____

180 In triangle *DEF*, the degree measure of angle *D* is 40° less than the degree measure of angle *E*, and 50° less than that of angle *F*.

What is the measure of ∠ D? _____

181 In quadrilateral *MNOP*, the degree measure of angle *N* is 40° more than the degree measure of angle *M*, and 20° less than that of angle *O*. Angle *P* measures 80°.

What is the measure of ∠ M? _____

182 In quadrilateral QRST, angle *Q* has a measure of *n* degrees. Angle *R* measures 10° more than angle *Q*. The measure of angle *S* is 10° more than that of angle *R*. Angle *T* measures 10° more than angle *S*.

What is the measure of ∠ Q? _____

Angles & Figures

○ ○ ○ ○ ○ ○ ○ ○ ○ ○ ○ ○ ○ ○ ○ ○

 One of my angles measures 90°. My other two angles are complementary.

What kind of triangle am I? _____

 All my sides are the same length and all my angles measure 108°.

What kind of polygon am I? _____

 My opposite angles have equal measures. My consecutive angles are supplementary. None are right angles. All my sides are congruent.

What kind of polygon am I? _____

 I have three sides. One of my angles measures 15°. Another has a measure of 60°.

What kind of triangle am I? _____

 I have six faces. Each face has the same surface area.

What kind of figure am I? _____

 The measures of all the angles in each of my two parallel bases total 720°. My other faces are rectangles.

What kind of figure am I? _____

5-Minute Math Problem of the Day Scholastic Professional Books

Surface Area

189 Twenty-seven small cubes are stacked to make this block. The entire block is painted red.

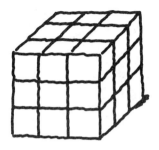

How many cubes are painted on one side? _____

How many cubes are painted on two sides? _____

How many cubes are painted on three sides?_____

How many cubes are unpainted?_____

190 Sixty-four small cubes are stacked to make this block. The entire block is painted blue.

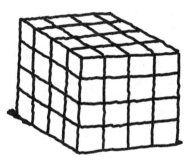

How many cubes are painted on one side? _____

How many cubes are unpainted?_____

191 Thirty-six small cubes are stacked to make this rectangular prism. The whole prism is painted green.

How many cubes are painted on three sides?_____

How many cubes are unpainted?_____

Pythagorean Theorem

192 Clark hikes 6 kilometers due east and then 8 kilometers due north. He stops to tie his hiking boots.

As the crow flies, how far is he from his starting point? _____

193 Elena jogs 7 kilometers due west and then 5 kilometers due south. She stops and checks her time.

As the crow flies, to the nearest kilometer, how far is she from her starting point?

_____

194 Warren walked 4 kilometers due east and then 5 kilometers due south. Next, he walked another 4 kilometers due east. Then he turned again, and walked 5 kilometers due south. He stopped there.

As the crow flies, to the nearest kilometer, how far is he from his starting point?

_____

195 Dana takes a shortcut home by walking diagonally across a rectangular park. The park measures 75 meters by 180 meters.

How much shorter is the route across the park than the route around its edge?

_____

5-Minute Math Problem of the Day Scholastic Professional Books

Percents, Fractions, & Decimals

 I am a percent that is equivalent to a fraction that is one-fourth of $\frac{1}{2}$.

What percent am I? _____

 I am a fraction that is equivalent to a decimal that is 15% less than 40%.

What fraction am I? _____

 I am a three-place decimal that is equivalent to the difference between 1 and $\frac{3}{8}$.

What decimal am I? _____

 I am a percent that is greater than 0.75. One of my digits is twice the other.

What percent am I? _____

 I am a two-place decimal that is greater than 25% and less than $\frac{2}{5}$. My tenths digit is a third of my hundredths digit.

What decimal am I? _____

 I am a lowest-terms fraction equivalent to a two-place decimal less than 0.5. The decimal's digits are 1 apart. Their sum is 9.

What fraction am I? _____

Percents & Measurement

 202

I am the number of feet in $66\frac{2}{3}\%$ of a yard.

What number am I? _____

 203

I am the number of pounds in 25% of a ton.

What number am I? _____

 204

I am the number of inches in 175% of a yard.

What number am I? _____

 205

I am the number of ounces in 75% of 2 pounds.

What number am I? _____

 206

I am the number of quarts in $33\frac{1}{3}\%$ of 6 gallons.

What number am I? _____

 207

I am the number of cups in $87\frac{1}{2}\%$ of 16 quarts.

What number am I? _____

Percents & Discounts

At Claude's Clothes there are never sales. But once merchandise arrives in the store, Claude takes 10% off the manufacturer's suggested price. He then slashes prices further, according to the following schedule:

Additional 25% off after 7 days in the store
Additional 50% off after 21 days in the store

208 A shipment of $120 sweaters arrives. Li buys one two weeks later.

What does she pay?_____

209 After 8 days in the store, a pair of jeans sells for $54.

What was its suggested price?_____

210 Eric bought a suit that had been on the rack for 24 days. He paid $135 for it.

What was its suggested price?_____

211 Mia bought two items at Claude's. Their combined manufacturer's price was $88, with one selling for $32 more than the other. When Mia made her purchase, the more expensive item had been in the store two weeks. The other item had been there for a month.

What did she pay in all?_____

Ratio & Proportion

212

Two numbers are in the ratio 2:3 and have sum of 25.

What are the numbers? _____

213

Two numbers are in the ratio 5:3. Their sum is 160.

What are the numbers? _____

214

Eighty Senators voted on a bill to allow unattended pets to enter supermarkets and shop for their own food. The bill passed by a ratio of 7 to 3.

How many voted for the bill? _____

215

In Erin's career on the basketball team, she made 7 of every 10 free throws. Last season, she attempted 60 free throws.

How many did she make? _____

216

Quinn, the quarterback, completed 60% of his 140 passes last season. This season he attempted twice as many passes. But he completed them at a rate that was two-thirds of what it had been the year before.

How many passes did he attempt?_____

How many did he complete?_____

217

Over his career, Gold Glove winner Boots Bupkis fielded without error 93.75% of the ground balls that came his way. In this year's playoffs, he fielded 32 balls with the same rate of success.

How many errors did he make? _____

218

Hannah's batting average was .400 after 60 at-bats. After 20 more times at bat, she lifted her average to .500.

How many hits did she get in those 20 at-bats? _____

5-Minute Math Problem of the Day Scholastic Professional Books

Counting Principle

 219 Rodney's band is currently planning a tour. They plan to play in Newburg, Newport, New Paltz, and Newly. But they can't decide on an order in which to visit those places.

How many choices do they have? _____

 220 In addition to the set of songs Rodney plans to play, he will read a poem, show a short video, and make a political speech. He knows that he will read his poem first, but hasn't yet decided the order of the other parts of the show.

How many orders are possible? _____

 221 Rodney can't make up his mind about what to wear on stage. So, he brings an assortment of clothing. He packs his blue suede shoes and his cowboy boots; his green suit, his yellow suit, and his pink suit; a white T-shirt, a red T-shirt, and a purple T-shirt; his top hat and his cowboy hat; and his polka dot bandanna. He'll wear that bandanna no matter what. He always wears a hat.

How many different outfits can he wear? _____

 222 At the last minute, Rodney decides that the blue suede shoes won't work. He leaves them home.

Now how many different outfits can Rodney put together for the tour? _____

Probability

 223 Lucy loves to wear gloves. She has four red gloves and two blue gloves in her drawer. They are not separated into pairs. One dark morning, she pulls out two gloves to wear to school. She puts on the gloves.

What is the probability that she is wearing a pair of...

blue gloves?_____

red gloves?_____

matching gloves?_____

 Suppose Lucy wants to make sure that when she reaches into her drawer, she is certain to take out enough gloves so that she will have one matching pair to wear.

How many gloves must she take?_____

 224 Kevin has ten socks with dots, ten socks with stripes, and ten orange socks in his drawer. Like Lucy's gloves, they are not paired. In the dark, Kevin reaches into the drawer without being able to see colors or designs. He chooses two socks.

What is the probability that he has chosen a pair of...

striped socks?_____

striped socks or orange socks?_____

 Suppose Kevin needs to have at least one pair of each kind of sock to take on a trip.

How many socks must he take?_____

5-Minute Math Problem of the Day Scholastic Professional Books

Patterns

225 A big bug ate 54 smaller bugs in 4 days. Each day, it ate 5 more bugs than it did on the previous day.

How many small bugs did the big bug eat on...

the first day? _____

the fourth day? _____

226 A huge frog ate 140 big bugs in 5 days. Each day, it ate 8 more bugs than it did on the previous day.

How many bugs did the frog eat on...

the first day? _____

the fifth day? _____

227 A little bug ate 135 tiny flies in 5 days. Each day, it ate 10 more flies than it did on the previous day.

How many flies had the bug eaten...

after three days? _____

after four days? _____

228 A cat pestered a mouse for the entire time the mouse lived in the basement: 6 days. Each day, it pestered the mouse 7 times more than it did the day before. In all, the cat annoyed the mouse 123 times.

How many times was the mouse pestered on the fourth day?

_____

Equations

 229

Patty is 3 times as old as her brother, Terry. In 10 years, the sum of their ages will be 36.

How old are they now? _____

 230

The sum of the ages of Mike and Dan is 20 years. In 4 years, Dan's age will be three-fourths of Mike's age.

How old is Mike now? _____

 231

The sum of the ages of Jasmine and her mother is 100. Thirty years ago, Jasmine's mother was 9 times as old as Jasmine was then.

How old is Jasmine now? _____

 232

The three Athios children have a combined age of 50. The youngest is half as old as the oldest. Ten years ago, the oldest was 7 times as old as the youngest.

How old were the children 10 years ago? _____

5-Minute Math Problem of the Day Scholastic Professional Books

Equations

233 Naomi caught half as many fish as Jack did. Together they caught 18 fish.

How many fish did Jack catch? _____

234 Karim caught $2\frac{1}{2}$ times as many fish as Ralph did. Together they caught 28 fish.

How many fish did Ralph catch? _____

235 Selena caught a fish that weighed $1\frac{3}{4}$ pounds. It weighed half a pound more than one-half the weight of the fish Sam caught.

What did Sam's fish weigh? _____

236 Miguel caught a fish after 2 hours, 30 minutes. That was 10 minutes less than four times as long as it took Shiretta to catch one.

How long did it take Shiretta? _____

Averages

237 Jenny's mean score on three science tests was 75. Her last two scores were 79 and 80. She forgot her score on the first test.

What was it? _____

238 Wanda wants to have a test average of 90 on her four French exams. On the first three tests, she got scores of 84, 96, and 85.

What does she need on the last test to reach her goal?

_____

239 In Dave's Latin class, tests count twice as heavily as quizzes. On the two tests he has taken, his scores were 70 and 85. He is taking a quiz this week.

What score does he need to get in order to bring his exam average up to 80? _____

240 Carla is in Dave's Latin class. On the two tests, she scored 80 and 86. After taking the quiz, her exam average was 85.

What score did she get on the quiz? _____

5-Minute Math Problem of the Day Scholastic Professional Books

Integers

 241 The sum of two integers is zero. The difference of the same two integers is 16.

What are the integers?_____

 242 Three consecutive integers have a sum of –15.

What are the integers?_____

 243 Two integers have a difference of 6 and a sum of –18.

What are the integers?_____

 244 A building built in 125 BC was totally destroyed in an earthquake in 404 AD.

For how many years had it stood?_____

 245 Over a period of 6 hours, the temperature rose 4°F, rose 3°F more, dropped 2°F, rose 1°F, dropped 2°F, and then dropped 3°F more. The temperature at the end of the 6-hour period was –5°F.

What was the starting temperature?_____

 246 A snail is at the bottom of an 8-foot hole. Each day, it crawls up 3 feet, but slides back 2 feet.

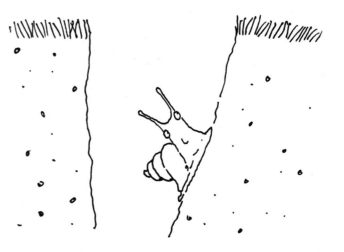

How many days will it take the snail to crawl out of the hole?_____

Squares & Square Roots

247
When the square root of one number is multiplied by the square root of a second number, the product is the square root of 36. One of the numbers is not 1.

What are the numbers? _____

248
When the square of one number is subtracted from the square of another, the difference is 1 less than the square of 9.

What are the numbers? _____

249
The sum of the square and the positive square root of a number is 84.

What is the number? _____

250
Two numbers are both less than the square of 10. One is the cube root of the other. When the positive square root of one of these numbers is added to the positive square root of the other number, the sum is the square root of a 3-digit number.

What are the numbers? _____

1. 9,875
2. 12,346
3. 93,876
4. 13,579
5. 951,876
6. 123,648
7. 5,562
8. 9,713
9. 35,283
10. 53,611
11. 3,462
12. 98,724
13. 8,749
14. 128,467
15. 617,823
16. 618,397
17. 65, 74
18. 550, 649
19. 7,500; 8,499
20. 85,000; 94,999
21. 69,500; 70,499
22. 165,000; 174,999
23. 533
24. 2,666
25. 81,218
26. 39,999
27. 496, 23
28. 49, 63; or 43, 69
29. 23, 496; or
    26, 493; or
    93, 426; or
    96, 423

30. 732, 469
31. 23, 64, 97; or
    23, 67, 94; or
    24, 63, 97; or
    24, 67, 93; or
    27, 63, 94; or
    27, 64, 93
32. 674, 392
33. Asteroids, 24–23
34. Comets, 98–96
35. 22, 25
36. 14, 15
37. 29, 31
38. 44, 45, 46
39. 17, 19, 21
40. 13, 52
41. 49
42. 63
43. 330
44. 2,004
45. 22
46. 33
47. 44
48. 55
49. 4 x 71
50. 78 x 43 + 1
51. 143 x 8 – 7
52. 18 x 734, or
    18 x 743, or
    73 x 184, or
    74 x 183
53. 418 ÷ 71, or
    418 ÷ 73, or

471 ÷ 83, or
473 ÷ 81
54. 83 ÷ 17
55. 79
56. 3,649
57. 9,999; 999
58. 30,499; 20,499
59. 56
60. 84
61. 95
62. 301
63. 160, 250
64. 267
65. 35
66. 45
67. 56
68. 50
69. 60
70. 72
71. 12, 15; 60
72. 8, 12; 24
73. 9, 15; 3
74. 8, 12, 16; 4
75. 9:24 AM
76. 9:00 PM
77. 25
78. 61
79. 9,753.1
80. 0.13579
81. 59.731
82. 315.79

83. 713.59

84. 79.531

85. 5.614

86. 4.7174

87. 0.615

88. 50.3055

89. 241.6994

90. 0.64435

91. 4.234

92. 12.584

93. 114.925

94. 203.460

95. 16.4 mi

96. 89.8 km

97. 26 mi

98. 21.2, 3.92

99. 6.86, 14.14

100. 13.5, 4.5

101. $155.50, $55.50

102. $7.50

103. $7.50

104. $8.06

105. 3.5, 2.5

106. 4.25, 4

107. 0.6, 0.4

108. 4.8, 5.8

109. $\frac{5}{10}$

110. $\frac{12}{32}$

111. $\frac{14}{35}$

112. $\frac{12}{16}$

113. $\frac{2}{5}$, or $\frac{3}{7}$, or $\frac{5}{11}$

114. $\frac{12}{13}$

115. $\frac{3}{6}$, $\frac{6}{12}$

116. $\frac{3}{7}$

117. $\frac{3}{12}$, $\frac{12}{48}$

118. $\frac{9}{15}$, $\frac{15}{25}$

119. $\frac{8}{12}$, $\frac{12}{18}$

120. $\frac{2}{4}$, $\frac{4}{8}$; $\frac{4}{8}$, $\frac{8}{16}$

121. $\frac{3}{16}$

122. $\frac{4}{15}$, or $\frac{2}{7}$

123. $\frac{17}{24}$

124. $\frac{43}{48}$

125. $1\frac{19}{24}$

126. $4\frac{9}{12}$

127. $\frac{1}{2} + \frac{1}{8}$

128. $\frac{3}{4} - \frac{5}{8}$

129. $\frac{4}{6} - \frac{1}{3}$

130. $\frac{3}{5} + \frac{4}{10}$

131. $\frac{8}{8} - \frac{3}{4}$

132. $\frac{6}{9} - \frac{5}{12}$

133. 12

134. 8

135. 9

136. 31

137. 60

138. 36, 48

139. $\frac{3}{4}$, $1\frac{1}{2}$

140. $\frac{2}{3}$, $\frac{1}{4}$

141. $\frac{3}{4}$, $\frac{1}{6}$; or $\frac{2}{3}$, $\frac{1}{4}$

142. $\frac{9}{10}$, $\frac{2}{3}$

143. $1\frac{1}{2}$, $\frac{1}{6}$

144. $\frac{4}{5}$, $\frac{9}{10}$

145. 4 yr

146. 3 lb

147. 60

148. 20 lb

149. 3 n, 12 d

150. 8 d, 2 q

151. 15 n, 5 d, 15 q

152. $1.00, $1.50, $2.50

153. 48

154. 2.5

155. 8,000

156. 0

157. 11

158. 15,840

159. l = 60 in, w = 15 in

160. 5 cm

161. 4 ft

162. 2,400 sq yd

163. –128°F

164. 79

165. 415

166. 2 lb 3 oz, or 35 oz

167. 12:40 AM

168. 11:00 AM

169. 8:00 AM

170. 5:30 PM

171. $68.90

172. $156.00

173. Weekend rates

174. Daily rates

175. 11

176. 7:05 PM

177. 4:05 AM

178. 11

179. 35°

180. 30°

181. 60°

182. 75°

183. right triangle

184. regular pentagon

185. rhombus

186. obtuse triangle

187. cube

188. hexagonal prism

189. 6, 12, 8, 1

190. 24, 8

191. 8, 2

192. 10 km

193. 9 km

194. 13 km

195. 60 m

196. $12\frac{1}{2}$%

197. $\frac{1}{4}$

198. 0.625

199. 84%

200. 0.26, or 0.39

201. $\frac{9}{20}$

202. 2

203. 500

204. 63

205. 24

206. 8

207. 56

208. $81

209. $80

210. $400

211. $49.95

212. 10, 15

213. 100, 60

214. 56

215. 42

216. 280, 112

217. 2

218. 16

219. 24

220. 6

221. 36

222. 18

223. $\frac{1}{15}$, $\frac{2}{5}$, $\frac{7}{15}$; 3

224. $\frac{3}{29}$, $\frac{6}{29}$; 22

225. 6, 21

226. 12, 44

227. 51, 88

228. 24

229. 12, 4

230. 12

231. 34

232. 14, 4, 2

233. 12

234. 8

235. $2\frac{1}{2}$ lb

236. 40 min

237. 66

238. 95

239. 90

240. 93

241. +8, –8

242. –4, –5, –6

243. –6, –12

244. 529

245. –6°F

246. 6

247. 4, 9

248. ±12, ±8

249. 9

250. 64, 4

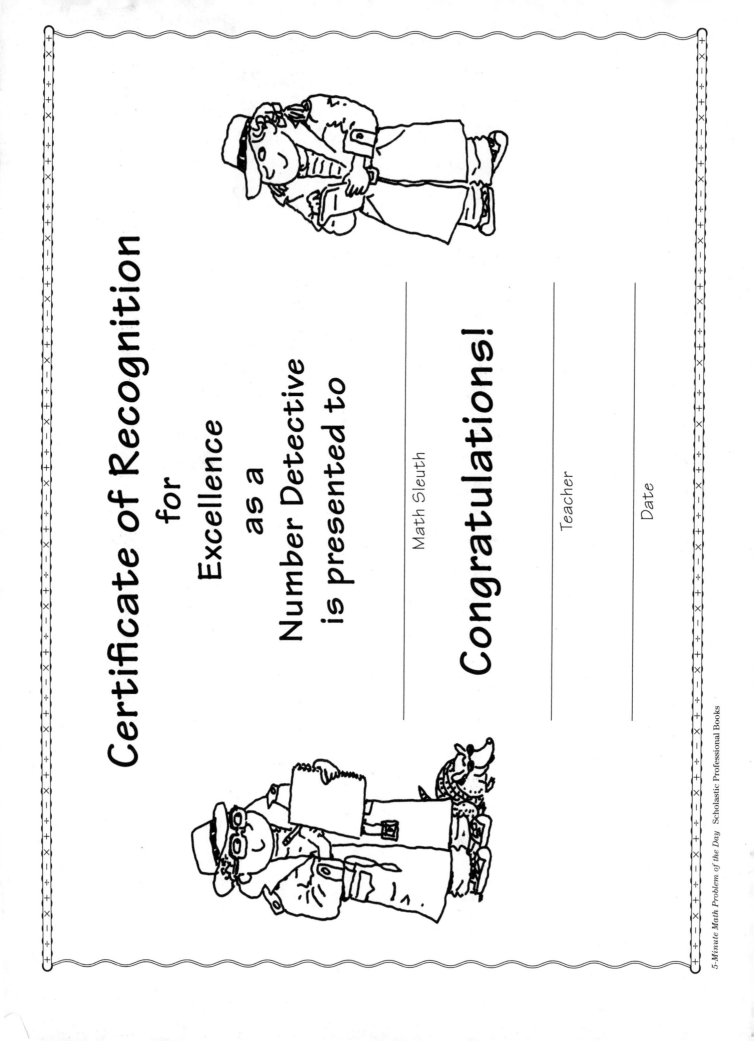

Certificate of Recognition

for
Excellence
as a
Number Detective

is presented to

_____

Math Sleuth

Congratulations!

_____

Teacher

_____

Date